AF228329

Hunting and Fishing

Small Game Hunting

Diane Bailey

Lerner Publications ◆ Minneapolis

Lerner Publications Company
An imprint of Lerner Publishing Group, Inc.
241 First Avenue North
Minneapolis, MN 55401 USA

For reading levels and more information, look up this title at www.lernerbooks.com.

Main body text set in Adrianna Regular.
Typeface provided by Chank.

Library of Congress Cataloging-in-Publication Data

Names: Bailey, Diane, 1966–author.
Title: Small game hunting / Diane Bailey.
Description: Minneapolis : Lerner Publications , [2024] | Series: Searchlight books—Hunting and fishing | Includes bibliographical references and index. | Audience: Ages 8–11 | Audience: Grades 4–6 | Summary: "Small game hunting is hunting for small animals such as squirrels and rabbits. Readers will discover the basics of small game hunting. Then they will learn about hunting safely, conservation, and more"—Provided by publisher.
Identifiers: LCCN 2022043008 (print) | LCCN 2022043009 (ebook) | ISBN 9781728491592 (library binding) | ISBN 9798765603789 (paperback) | ISBN 9798765600559 (ebook)
Subjects: LCSH: Small game hunting—Juvenile literature.
Classification: LCC SK340 .B35 2024 (print) | LCC SK340 (ebook) | DDC 799.2/5—dc23/eng/20220921

LC record available at https://lccn.loc.gov/2022043008
LC ebook record available at https://lccn.loc.gov/2022043009

Manufactured in the United States of America
3-1010668-51108-2/13/2024

Table of Contents

Chapter 1

GOING SMALL GAME HUNTING

You stay perfectly still and quiet. The woods are quiet too. You listen very closely. Some leaves rustle softly. A stick breaks with a small pop. Then you see a flash of gray fur. Still, you wait a few moments longer. You wait until you have a good, clean shot.

Your patience pays off. In a moment, a squirrel scrambles into the open. Now it is time.

HUNTERS FIND MANY TYPES OF
SMALL GAME IN THE WOODS.

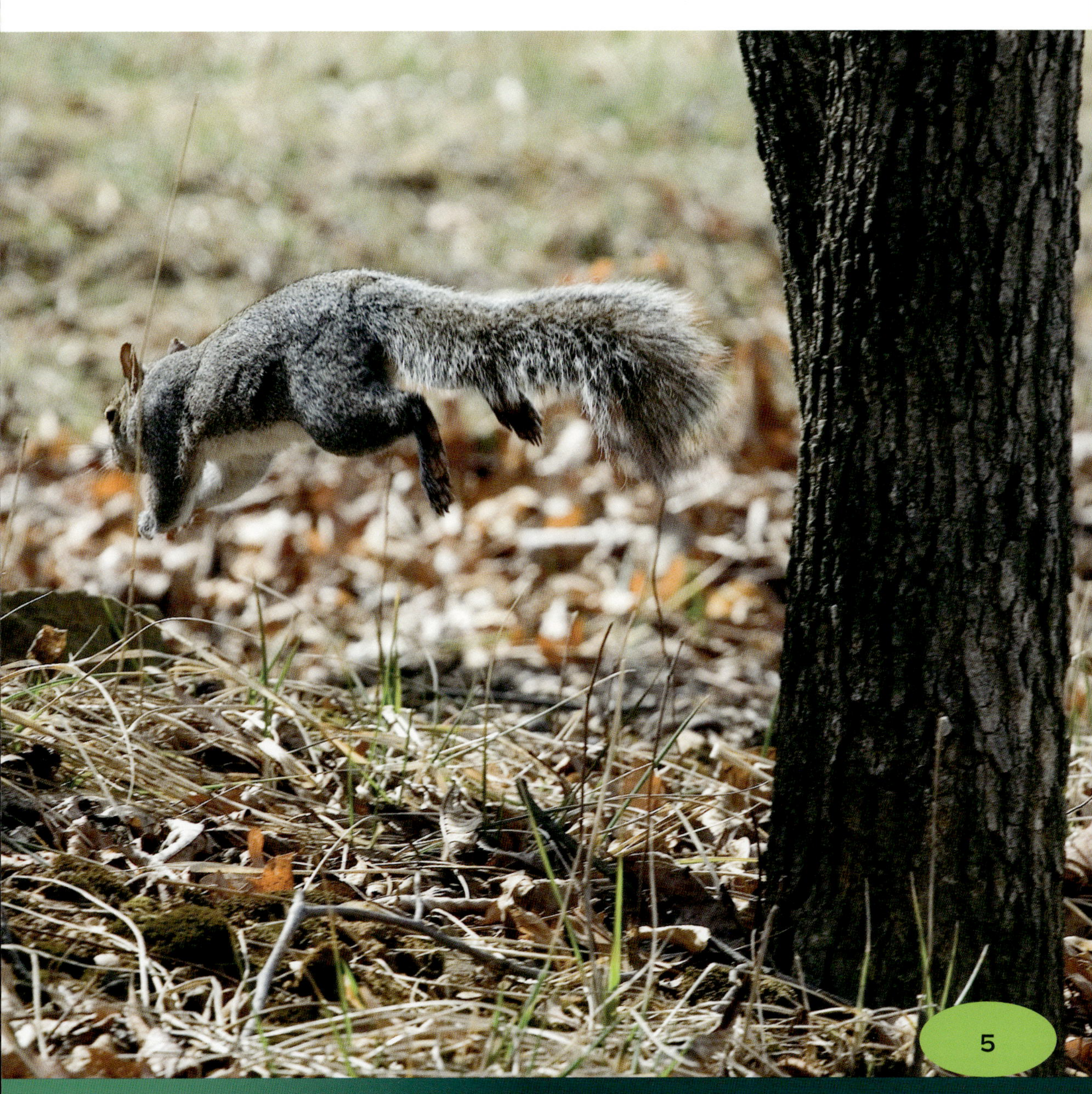

A rifle or shotgun scope helps hunters keep small game in focus.

Hunting Big and Small

Even big game hunters like to pursue small game. These animals usually weigh less than 40 pounds (18.1 kg). They are fast and it takes great aim to catch them. Squirrels, rabbits, hares, and many birds are common types of small game hunted for food and sport.

Rabbits are one of the most popular animals to hunt.

    Small game is also more plentiful than big game.
Hunters may find just one big animal such as deer in
a 20-acre area. But they are likely to find many small
animals in that same space.

Hunting History

In ancient times, hunters often focused on large animals like deer or buffalo because they provided the most meat. But when large game was scarce, it was harder to feed a community. Small game was a good backup since there was usually more of it. It was also possible for more people to help hunt, since catching small game was easier. People who were not strong enough to manage big animals could still handle smaller ones.

Ancient hunters hunted big game like bison.

Getting Ready

A reliable firearm, sturdy clothing, and safety gear are all part of a hunter's tool kit. Finding animals is the first step in hunting them, so some hunters also carry binoculars to spot animals. They might also set up trail cameras a few days in advance. The cameras show where animals are most active.

▲

Choosing a Weapon

Some hunters use a bow and arrow to hunt for small game, but most choose a shotgun or rifle. Beginners usually have better luck with a shotgun. Shotguns release a burst of many small pellets, called shot. The pellets scatter when they leave the gun. This spray of pellets is more likely to hit a target than a single rifle bullet.

A rifle requires more precise aim and is more difficult to shoot. However, rifle bullets are more powerful and travel farther. They are good for hunting larger animals. Some hunters use a shooting stick or bipod. These stands stop the gun from wobbling during a shot.

STAYING SAFE

Young hunters should always hunt with experienced trusted adults. A team of hunters can help one another if something goes wrong. Cell phones are one way to keep in contact. Using two-way radios offers a reliable backup plan in remote areas where cell phones don't work.

Trees start to look alike after a while. That's why smart hunters plan ahead so they don't get lost. If they're not familiar with an area, they look at a map first. They also take a compass with them and may mark the trail to remember the path they have taken.

Hunters don't just keep an eye out for animals. They must look for other people too. Hunters often wear bright, orange vests and caps. This safety clothing is used, and often required, so that hunters don't mistake other hunters for game.

STEM Spotlight

People's eyes recognize three colors—red, green, and blue. Our brains then mix those colors together to see even more colors. Most mammals, however, only recognize two colors, like blue and yellow or blue and green. They can't mix those together to see orange, so they don't notice the blaze orange clothing worn by hunters. Instead, animals depend on sound, smell, and movement to tell them who's around.

Bright orange clothes keep hunters visible to other hunters.

It's important to practice using a firearm before using one on a hunt.

Using a Firearm

Taking a hunter education class is the first step for any hunter. Being able to load, unload, and carry a gun safely is essential for all hunters. Hunters learn not to walk on rough ground or cross fences with a loaded gun. They also learn to never point a gun at someone else. These classes also teach skills like how to track and attract animals.

In the Zone

It is best to hunt in groups of three or fewer hunters. Hunters should space themselves about 25 to 40 yards (22.7 to 36.6 m) apart. Each hunter's zone of fire reaches out about 45 degrees in front of them. It is the area where it is safe to shoot. That is their zone of fire.

Hunters spend hours at target practice before they ever take a shot at a live animal. This makes them comfortable and confident using the gun. It also improves their aim, so they can make a clean kill shot. That way, the animal won't suffer.

LEARNING TO HUNT SMALL GAME TAKES LOTS OF SHOOTING PRACTICE.

ON THE HUNT

Hunters always ask one question: Where is the best place to hunt? The answer always changes because it depends on several things. What type of animal are they hunting? When is the official hunting season? What is the weather like? For the best chance of success, a small game hunter must be flexible!

Habits and Habitats

Small game hunters study animal habitats and behavior. Just like people, different animals like different things. Rabbits like to hang out in woody brush. Squirrels eat nuts, so they can be found in forests with hardwood trees like oak, walnut, and hickory. Groundhogs prefer fields and the edges of forests, but they sometimes climb trees.

Looking for Clues

Many wild animals stay home during the middle of the day. They look for food at dawn and dusk, when the light is not as bright, and they can see better. These are also the best times to avoid predators.

Animals leave clues that they've been around. They chew and scratch tree bark, leaving marks behind. They also leave behind scat, or poop. Hunting by looking for these types of signs is called tracking.

Stand Still

Hunters pursue animals slowly and quietly when still hunting. A big part of still hunting is waiting. A hunter looking for prey may stand still for a couple of minutes, listening and waiting. If nothing appears, he moves just a few steps, slowly and quietly, and tries a new spot. Moving around a lot or making too much noise is a sure way to scare off game. A still hunter may not move more than the length of a football field in an entire hour!

Still hunters wait for prey to come their way.

A Hunter's Best Friend

Some hunters use dogs to help find and trap their prey. Thanks to their excellent sense of smell, dogs can find prey that humans cannot. A dog's job is to bring the prey and hunter together. For example, a dog might chase a squirrel into a tree and keep it there until the hunter arrives. They might also flush prey such as birds. They bark and run into brush where birds are hiding to scare them into the open, where the hunter is waiting.

Hunting History

Dogs are great hunting companions. The ancient Greeks and Egyptians raised dogs to help with hunting. So did early Europeans. Hounds were popular because of their keen sense of smell. Spaniels were good at flushing small game from thick brush. Breeding dogs back then took a lot of time and money and was mostly for rich people. Now, many hunters use dogs for hunting.

Spaniels are still popular hunting dogs.

Chapter 4

HUNTING AND CONSERVATION

Most hunters believe in conservation. They work to preserve animals and the environment. It makes sense because no animals means no hunting.

To make sure there are always enough animals, most can only be hunted during certain times of year. That is when they are in season. Mating animals and babies are always off-limits. There is also a bag limit, the number of animals a hunter can take in a day.

Officials keep track of animal populations to keep nature balanced. Allowing for too much hunting can deplete a species. With too little hunting, animal populations can grow to the point where one species threatens other species. The goal is to keep animal populations at just the right size.

Pesky Pests

An exception to animal control is varmints, or animals that are pests. There is usually no limit on them. Varmints can carry diseases and may kill farmers' livestock for food. Rats, groundhogs, prairie dogs, foxes, and coyotes are often considered varmints.

STEM Spotlight

Animals, plants, and bugs evolve to live in certain places. But sometimes they get into other areas and take over. These invasive species are hard on the species that already live there. Even tiny bacteria or plants can be a big problem. They can stick to people's cars, clothes, or shoes. It's a good idea to rinse your shoes and car tires before moving into new areas and wash your clothes. This helps prevent the spread of invasive species.

Kudzu is an aggressive invasive species.

Protecting the Environment

All hunters must buy a license from their state. This gives them permission to hunt. The state then uses this money to preserve animal habitats. For example, they might plant trees or clean up the water supply.

Hunters must also practice good habits when they're out. Good conservation helps keep the environment stable for all species. If everyone works together, hunters can enjoy the land now and in the future.

Hunting licenses help pay for conservation efforts.

Hunting Hints

- Plan a pre-hunting trip to learn the landscape and observe animal habits.

- Go out at dawn or dusk when animals are more active.

- Look for "parts" of an animal, like a tail or paw, to find animals in hiding.

- Stand so the wind is blowing away from your prey and toward you. This helps disguise your smell.

- While hunting, take several quick small steps to move from place to place. You'll sound less human!

Animals are good at hiding in plain sight.

Glossary

bipod: a stand that holds a gun

conservation: protecting resources like land and water and using them wisely

flush: to force game from cover

game: animals hunted for food or sport

habitat: the environment a particular animal lives in

invasive species: an animal or plant that lives where it is not native and causes harm

population: the total number of a type of animal

scat: animal droppings

stalking: to follow signs leading to a particular type of game or group of animals

still hunting: to look for animals slowly and quietly

tracking: stealthily approaching prey that has already been seen

zone of fire: the area that each hunter in a group may shoot in

Learn More

Brach, Kyle. *Bowhunting*. Minneapolis: Lerner Books, 2024.

Britannica Kids: Hunting
    https://kids.britannica.com/students/article/hunting/274993

Doyle, Abby Badach. *Small Game Hunting*. New York: Gareth Stevens
    Publishing, 2023.

How Stuff Works: How Sport Hunting Works
    https://adventure.howstuffworks.com/outdoor-activities/hunting/
    alternative-methods/sport-hunting.htm

Kiddle: Hunting Dog Facts for Kids
    https://kids.kiddle.co/Hunting_dog

Uhl, Xina M. and Judy Monroe Peterson. *Insider Tips for Hunting Small
    Game*. New York: Rosen Central, 2019.

Index

Photo Acknowledgments

Image Credits: p. 5; Guy Sagi/Shutterstock, p. 6; krasula/Dreamstime, p. 6; Joe Gough/Shutterstock, p.8; Seagrave/Dreamstime, p. 9; Danus Strazdas/Dreamstime, p. 10; Komilovdream/Dreamstime, p. 11; Georgii Shipin/Shutterstock, p. 13; Jordi Mora Igual/Dreamstime, p. 14; ElvK/Shutterstock, p. 15; Roman Chazov/Shutterstock, p. 16; Steven Oehlenschlager/Shutterstock, p. 17; Feverpitched/iStock Photos, p. 19; George Burba/Dreamstime, p. 20; Natalia Sokko/Dreamstime, p. 21; CSNafzger/Shutterstock; p. 22; Modestil/Dreamstime, p. 23; Freefrei/Shutterstock, p. 25; engel.ac/Shutterstock, p. 26; Nhut Nguyen/Shutterstock, p. 27; Christie S Simpson/Shutterstock, p.28; Mega Pixel/Shutterstock, p. 29; Cora Mueller/Shutterstock.

Cover: ZoranOrcik/Shutterstock.